How many mice make an ELEPHANT?

and other BIG QUESTIONS About SIZE and DISTANCE

**To anyone who thinks numbers can't be fun,
and all animal lovers—T.T.**

**To Cian & Fionn, whose curiosity inspires me to be better.
Keep asking questions—A.C.**

A Raspberry Book
Editorial: Kathryn Jewitt
Art direction & cover design: Sidonie Beresford-Browne
Internal design: Kim Hankinson
Consultant: Mike Goldsmith

KINGFISHER
LONDON & NEW YORK

Text and design copyright © Raspberry Books Ltd 2020
First published 2020 in the United States by Kingfisher,
120 Broadway, New York, NY 10271
Kingfisher is an imprint of Macmillan Children's Books, London
All rights reserved.

Distributed in the U.S. and Canada by Macmillan,
120 Broadway, New York, NY 10271

Library of Congress Cataloging-in-Publication Data has been applied for.

ISBN: 978-0-7534-7565-2

Kingfisher books are available for special promotions and premiums.
For details contact: Special Markets Department, Macmillan, 120 Broadway,
New York, NY 10271

For more information, please visit
www.kingfisherbooks.com

Printed in China
1 3 5 7 9 8 6 4 2
1TR/0320/UG/WKT/128MA

How many mice make an ELEPHANT?

and other BIG Questions About SIZE and DISTANCE

By
Tracey Turner

With Some Notes About Numbers by Kjartan Poskitt

Illustrated by Aaron Cushley

KINGFISHER
LONDON & NEW YORK

CONTENTS

Introduction

Have you ever wondered...

...just how big an elephant is?

Or how many flights of stairs it would take to climb Mount Everest?

Well, help is at hand, because we're about to find out. On the way, we'll...

...scale the world's tallest building using giraffes

...squash a lot of astronauts inside the International Space Station

...fill a stadium with soccer balls

...weigh a goldfish

...and meet an iceberg the size of Jamaica.

In addition to finding out about size and what fits into what how many times, you might discover some unexpected facts about things like blue whales' earwax, the moons of Jupiter, and kangaroos the size of grapes.

With elephants and mountains featuring in this book, you won't be surprised to hear that we'll be meeting some very, very big numbers. But don't let that worry you! There's a note about numbers by Kjartan Poskitt, author of the Murderous Math book series, on page 8, and his guide to different measurements and how to measure is on page 44.

Plus, as if all that weren't enough, you will be flying around at 500 mph to some interesting destinations using your very own jetpack.

But first, turn the page and let Kjartan set your mind at rest about big numbers.

Say HELLO to BIG NUMBERS

By Kjartan Poskitt

Big numbers might look scary at first, but when you know how they work, they're fun!

Let's start by looking at a big number you might find at home. How many drops of water do you think it takes to fill a bathtub all the way to the top?

Let's look at the sums.

- 1,000 — one thousand
- 10,000 — ten thousand
- 100,000 — one hundred thousand
- 1,000,000 — one million
- 10,000,000 — ten million

A full bathtub holds *about* 60 gallons of water, and each gallon of water is *about* 80,000 drops. Therefore the total number of drops in the bathtub is:

60 x 80,000 = 4,800,000

You'll notice we said *about*. When we play with very big numbers, we don't usually need to be absolutely accurate, and that means it makes the sums simpler to do. The main thing is to make sure you have the right number of zeros!

When we work out 60 x 80,000, we first add up the number of zeros. We get 1 + 4 = five zeros. Remember that!

Now we ignore the zeros and just multiply the numbers at the front. 6 x 8 = 48.

Now we just put our five zeros on the end of the 48. We get the answer 4800000, and, when you put the commas in, it becomes 4,800,000. So there are *about* five million drops of water in the bathtub!

Here are some more to take a guess at:

- What's longer—a million seconds or 1 year?
- What's taller—100 giraffes or 1,000,000 ants?
- What's heavier—the water in an Olympic swimming pool or the Eiffel Tower?

You'll find the answers at the back of the book.

Using a Calculator

Calculators are really good for big sums *unless you push the wrong buttons.* It won't be the calculator's fault if you get the wrong answer! Therefore, it's always good to have a rough answer in your head and make sure the calculator agrees with you.

Suppose a bakery makes 873 boxes of cookies with 23 cookies in each box. How many cookies is that altogether? The sum is 873 x 23, but which answer do you think is correct?

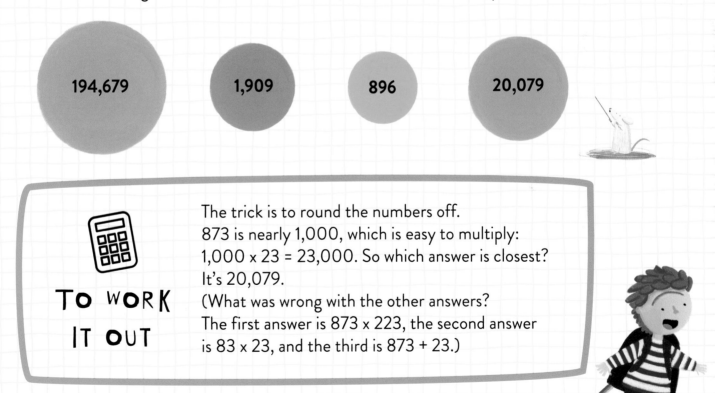

194,679   **1,909**   **896**   **20,079**

TO WORK IT OUT

The trick is to round the numbers off.
873 is nearly 1,000, which is easy to multiply:
1,000 x 23 = 23,000. So which answer is closest?
It's 20,079.
(What was wrong with the other answers?
The first answer is 873 x 223, the second answer is 83 x 23, and the third is 873 + 23.)

It's fun guessing what the answer to a big sum will be, and then using a calculator to see how close you were. The more often you try it, the better you will be!

Playing around with big numbers tells us all kinds of amazing and crazy things. So are you ready? Off we go . . .

How Many mice Make an ELEPHANT?

You have probably already noticed that elephants are very big and mice are very small. In fact, African elephants are the biggest land animal in the world. But how many mice could you fit into one of these hefty, trumpeting stompers?

This enormous African elephant takes up around **350,000 cubic inches** (cu. in.) of space, which is about **200 cubic feet** (cu. ft.).

This little house mouse takes up around **1.5 cubic inches** (cu. in.) of space, or **0.00087 cubic feet** (cu. ft.).

TO WORK IT OUT

Divide 350,000 by 1.5. (Or **divide 200 by 0.00087** if you'd rather use cubic feet). The results are similar.

You'd need about 230,000 mice to fill up the space of just one elephant!

one at a time

How Small is Our Mouse?

WEIGHT
about 1 ounce

LENGTH
about 3 in. (body)
about 2.75 in. (tail)

How Big is Our Elephant?

WEIGHT
about 6 tons, or 12,000 pounds

HEIGHT
about 11 ft.

Even though they're tiny, house mice can jump up to 18 in. high. That's like you leaping up to the roof of a house. Elephants can't jump at all—they never have all four feet off the ground at the same time.

An elephant uses its trunk for many things, including sniffing, picking things up, sucking up water to drink, sucking up mud or sand for a bath, and giving other elephants a hug. The trunk has more than 40,000 muscles to help it do all these jobs. About 24 house mice could line up along an African elephant's trunk.

You could wrap yourself up inside an elephant's ear, which is about 6 ft. across—as long as the elephant didn't mind, of course.

There are *billions* of house mice in the world, but not so many African elephants. Today there are about 415,000 African elephants in the wild, but 100 years ago there were more than three million of them.

How many flights of stairs to the top of MOUNT EVEREST?

Grab your crampons and an ice pick, because it's time to scale the highest mountain in the world. Obviously, it would be a lot easier if there were stairs to climb to the top, but how many flights would we need?

The flight of stairs in our imaginary house is **8 ft.** high.

Mount Everest is **29,029 ft.** high.

We would need **3,628 FLIGHTS OF STAIRS** (plus a few steps) to climb Mount Everest!

IS THERE AN ELEVATOR?

TO WORK IT OUT

Divide 29,029 by 8

12

Here is the highest peak on each continent, along with the number of flights of stairs needed to climb it. Australia's Mount Kosciuszko is just a hill compared to Everest!

1. **ASIA:** Mount Everest 29,029 ft.   (**3,629** flights of stairs)
2. **SOUTH AMERICA:** Aconcagua 22,841 ft.   (**2,855** flights of stairs)
3. **NORTH AMERICA:** Denali 20,308 ft.   (**2,538** flights of stairs)
4. **AFRICA:** Mount Kilimanjaro 19,340 ft.   (**2,417** flights of stairs)
5. **EUROPE:** Mount Elbrus 18,510 ft.   (**2,314** flights of stairs)
6. **ANTARCTICA:** Vinson Massif 16,050 ft.   (**2,006** flights of stairs)
7. **AUSTRALIA:** Mount Kosciuszko 7,310 ft.   (**914** flights of stairs)

All five of the world's highest peaks are found in the Himalaya range, which includes more than 50 peaks that are higher than 23,000 ft., and 11 peaks over 26,000 ft.

Mount Everest was climbed for the first time in 1953 (at least, the first time it was recorded). Since then there have been more than 7,000 ascents, and there are hundreds more every year.

May and June are the only months that weather allows climbers to reach Everest's summit, and sometimes there's a long line of mountaineers waiting to get there!

The Himalayas formed when two massive plates in Earth's crust collided with one another, joining India (which used to be a very big island off the coast of Australia) with Asia. India drifted slowly northward until it crashed into Asia about 40 to 50 million years ago.

How many swimming pools in the OCEAN?

There's more ocean in the world than there is land, and while some of it is shallow enough to wade in, a great deal of it is very deep indeed. Just how much seawater is sloshing around on planet Earth compared to how much there is in a pool?

We're using an **Olympic-sized swimming pool** that contains **90,000 cu. ft.** of water.

There's a lot of water in the ocean—around **50,000,000,000,000,000,000 cu. ft.** (That's 50 quintillion cu. ft.)

There are about 556,000,000,000,000 **(THAT'S 556 TRILLION)** swimming pools' worth of water in the ocean!

TO WORK IT OUT

Divide 50,000,000,000,000,000,000 by 90,000 (there are too many zeros to fit on a calculator, so use the zero counting method on page 8, but subtract zeros instead of adding them.)

Unlike a swimming pool, the ocean is salty—the salt comes from rocks on land as rainwater erodes them and washes into the sea, and also from minerals in geothermal vents on the seafloor.

On average, the sea is 2.29 mi. deep, but the deepest part is the Mariana Trench in the Pacific Ocean. The deepest area of the trench, called Challenger Deep, is nearly 7 mi. (or more than 13 Burj Khalifa skyscrapers—see pages 16–17) below the sea's surface. Three expeditions have been made to the freezing, dark, bone-crushingly pressurized trench—the latest in 2019.

MOUNT EVEREST WOULD COME UP TO HERE

Although the oceans all join up, they're usually divided into four main oceans—the Pacific, Atlantic, Indian, and Arctic. Some people call the water around Antarctica the Southern Ocean, making five in total.

30%

The ocean is our planet's largest habitat, covering 70% of its surface.

The Pacific Ocean is the biggest—it contains half of all the seawater on Earth.

If the base of **Mount Everest** was at the bottom of the **Mariana Trench**, there would be more than **1.25 mi. of clear water** above the top of the mountain.

HOW many GIRAFFES make the tallest SKYSCRAPER?

We're using this lovely giraffe. She's named Gillian, and she's **15 ft.** tall.

If you're afraid of heights, you might need to close your eyes and hang on to something sturdy. How many giraffes would have to stand on top of one another to get to the top of the world's tallest building?

The Burj Khalifa is the world's tallest building—it's a dizzying **2,717 ft.** tall.

You'd need about 181 **GILLIAN-SIZED GIRAFFES**, stacked very uncomfortably one on top of the other, to reach the **TOP OF THE BURJ KHALIFA.**

To WORK IT OUT

Divide 2,717 by 15

Giraffes are the world's tallest mammals, between about 13 ft. and 20 ft. tall. Just their necks are longer than most grown-ups, and their blue tongues can measure more than 20 in.

The World's Tallest Buildings Measured in Giraffes

1. **BURJ KHALIFA,** United Arab Emirates   **181 GIRAFFES** (2,717 ft.)
2. **SHANGHAI TOWER,** China   **138 GIRAFFES** (2,074 ft.)
3. **MAKKAH ROYAL CLOCK TOWER,** Saudi Arabia   **131 GIRAFFES** (1,972 ft.)
4. **PING AN FINANCE CENTER,** China   **131 GIRAFFES** (1,965 ft.)
5. **LOTTE WORLD TOWER,** Korea   **121 GIRAFFES** (1,819 ft)

(Giraffe numbers have been rounded up or down—no giraffes have been harmed in the making of this book.)

From 1931 until 1972, the world's tallest building was the Empire State Building in New York City, at 1,250 ft., or 83 Gillians. You could stack two Empire State Buildings on top of one another and still have 217 ft. left to reach the top of the Burj Khalifa. New technology and lighter building materials mean buildings keep getting higher and higher.

The Burj Khalifa has to cope with the wind, like all tall buildings, and also with salty water in the ground that could damage its foundations. So its base is spread over a wide area, and its deep, concrete-and-metal foundations are resistant to saltwater.

Steel frames help support the thousands of tons that today's tall buildings weigh.

17

How many SANDBOXES in the SAHARA DESERT?

The Sahara is the world's biggest sandy desert—it is almost as big as China. If all the sand somehow blew away suddenly, how many sandboxes would we need to refill it?

> Do you have a BIGGER WHEELBARROW?

> There's roughly **7 quadrillion cu. ft. (7,000,000,000,000,000 cu. ft.)** of sand in the Sahara.

> This beautiful sandbox contains **70 cu. ft.** of sand.

We need
100 TRILLION
(that's one followed
by 14 zeros) sandboxes
to fill the Sahara.
I hope you have
a wheelbarrow!

TO WORK IT OUT

Divide 7,000,000,000,000,000 by 70 (there are too many zeros to fit on a calculator, so use the zero counting method on page 8, but subtract the zeros instead of adding them.)

The Sahara is 3.6 million sq. mi. of dry, dusty desert. The island of Mauritius off the coast of Africa could fit into it 4,600 times! Most of the Sahara is gravelly and rocky, with mountains up to 11,302 ft. high, but there's still plenty of sand—around 770,000 sq. mi. (which we're saying is 330 ft. deep on average to come up with our volume).

Saharan sand dunes are called ergs and can be 600 ft. high, though that's nowhere near the tallest in the world. The tallest can measure over 3,000 ft.

The Sahara has extreme temperatures: it's often around 100°F during the day, but the highest temperature ever recorded was 136°F. On winter nights the temperature can fall below freezing.

Anywhere on Earth that gets less than 10 in. of rain in a year is a desert, so not all deserts are hot and sandy. The biggest ones of all are Antarctica and the Arctic, planet Earth's cold poles.

Some Very Big Deserts

. . . and how many times the country of France could fit into them

1.	SAHARA	3.6 MILLION sq. mi. (just over 14.5 x France)
2.	ARABIAN	888,000 sq. mi. (just over 3.5 x France)
3.	GOBI	502,000 sq. mi. (just over 2 x France)
4.	KALAHARI	347,000 sq. mi. (just over 1.6 x France)
5.	PATAGONIAN	240,000 sq. mi. (just over 1.1 x France)

How many HIGH JUMPS to the MOON?

Even the world-record-holding high jumper couldn't get anywhere near the Moon, which is a pretty long way away. But how many jumps would it take?

The distance to the Moon varies quite a bit, but a rough average is about **240,000 mi.**, or about **1,300,000,000 (1.3 billion) ft.**

The world record high jump is **8 ft. 0.46 in.** (roughly 8.04 ft.), jumped by Javier Sotomayor from Cuba in 1993.

On average, the Moon is **161,691,542 AND A BIT HIGH JUMPS AWAY** from Earth! Only nursery rhyme cows are capable of jumping over it.

TO WORK IT OUT
Divide 1,300,000,000 by 8.04

It's just as well we don't have to rely on jumping to get into space—we use rockets to zoom us up there instead. During the 1960s and '70s, NASA's Apollo program sent nine missions to the Moon, and altogether twelve astronauts have walked on its surface.

The Moon is roughly a quarter of the size of Earth at 2,160 mi. in diameter. If you hollowed out Earth, there would be room for about 50 of our Moons (if they were all squashed in).

Moons in Our Solar System

Earth only has one moon, but some planets in our solar system have several.

- MERCURY AND VENUS: 0
- EARTH: 1
- MARS: 2
- JUPITER: 79 (the biggest planet also has the biggest moon, Ganymede)
- SATURN: at least 82 (astronomers keep finding more and more!)
- URANUS: 27
- NEPTUNE: 14

The Moon has only one-sixth of Earth's gravity, so you'd weigh a lot less and be able to jump six times higher on the Moon. If Sotomayor had completed his record-breaking jump on the Moon instead of on Earth, he could have jumped over a three-story building.

Human high-jumping efforts are pathetically puny compared to how high some animals can jump. White-tailed jackrabbits have been recorded jumping as high as 21 ft., which would be like you jumping over a giraffe.

Fleas jump up to 200 times their body length—like you jumping over 24 buses parked end to end.

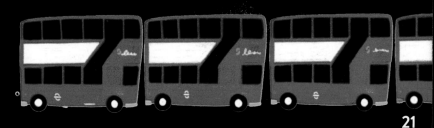

HOW MANY KANGAROO HOPS to cross AUSTRALIA?

Australia is the name of a continent as well as a country. Kangaroos are some of its most famous animals, known for their awesome hopping abilities. If a kangaroo hopped across the entire width of Australia, how many hops would it need to make?

The distance across Australia from east to west is roughly **2,500 mi.**, or **13,200,000 ft.**

Our red kangaroo covers **25 ft.** in one hop.

It would take 528,000 **KANGAROO HOPS TO CROSS AUSTRALIA.** Maybe a bunch of kangaroos could do it in a relay.

TO WORK IT OUT

Divide 13,200,000 by 25

As well as covering 25 ft. across the ground, a red kangaroo's hop can reach 6 ft. high—it could jump over you with no problem at all. A kangaroo can reach speeds of up to 35 mph as it bounds along, breaking the speed limit in a town or city.

The World's Four Widest Countries Measured in Kangaroo Hops

Australia isn't the widest country in the world—Canada is. You could fit more than two Australias side by side, going east to west, across the width of Canada. All the following numbers are just rough estimates. Especially for the kangaroos.

1. **Canada**   1.22 million kangaroo hops (5,800 mi. wide)
2. **Russia**   1.18 million kangaroo hops (5,600 mi. wide)
3. **China**   676,000 kangaroo hops (3,200 mi. wide)
4. **USA**   591,000 kangaroo hops (2,800 mi. wide)

Marsupials are a type of mammal. After a baby marsupial is born, it lives in its mother's pouch until it's bigger. The red kangaroo is the biggest marsupial of all. A baby red kangaroo is only the size of a grape when it's born, but it grows into a whopping great hopper with a body length of up to 5.25 ft., plus a tail that's more than 3 ft. long.

The main part of Australia is an island, but the country includes other smaller islands, too. The biggest is Tasmania, which is 200 mi., or 42,240 kangaroo hops, from east to west.

How many ICE CUBES make an ICEBERG?

Icebergs are enormous chunks of ice floating in the ocean or a lake. Ice cubes are for keeping your lemonade cold. But they're both made of the same thing—frozen water. We know icebergs are big, but how many ice cubes make one?

Our medium-size iceberg is about the size of a big house, at **14,000 cu. ft.**, or about **24,000,000 cu. in.** (that's **24 million cu. in.**).

Our ice cubes have a volume of **1.5 cu. in.**

ICE CAFE

There are **16 MILLION ICE CUBES IN OUR ICEBERG.** You could keep everyone in New Zealand's drinks cold with that.

 **TO WORK IT OUT**

Divide 24,000,000 by 1.5. We are going to need quite a lot of ice cubes.

A chunk of floating ice is called an iceberg once it's bigger than 16 ft. across. Chunks of floating ice that are smaller than that are known as bergy bits and growlers. You'll notice that most of our iceberg is underwater, and this is true of all of them—usually you can only see about a tenth of an iceberg above the surface.

Icebergs come in different shapes and sizes, from house-size chunks to ice islands. They form when they break off from glaciers, which are huge rivers of ice that flow very slowly across land.

Ice floats in water because it isn't as dense as liquid water. Icebergs are made from fresh water, which is less dense than salty seawater, and that helps them float, too.

Most glaciers are found in Antarctica and Greenland. Around 5.2 million sq. mi. of Antarctica is covered in glaciers, and if all of them melted, sea levels would rise by about 190 ft. Sea levels are rising, partly because of ice melting as Earth's climate gets warmer.

Iceberg B-15 was the biggest iceberg ever recorded. It measured almost 185 mi. long and 23 mi. wide—bigger than the island of Jamaica.

How many Christmas Trees make a coast REDWOOD?

Coast redwoods are the tallest trees in the world, and you will probably be surprised at just how tall they can get. Christmas trees need to be small enough to fit inside your house. How many small trees would you have to stand on top of one another to reach the top of a great big one?

Our Christmas tree is **7 ft.** tall (and honestly that's a bit on the big side for our living room).

This is the tallest coast redwood alive today, which also makes it the tallest tree alive today. It's **380 ft.** tall.

We need 54 CHRISTMAS TREES (plus a few branches) to reach the top of the coast redwood!

TO WORK IT OUT
Divide 380 by 7

Coast redwoods are one of about 60,000 different species of trees in the world. Several different species are used as Christmas trees, including Norway spruce, blue spruce, Fraser fir, and Scotch pine.

The tallest coast redwood is absolutely huge—as big as a 25-story building. It's 65 ft. taller than the Big Ben clock tower in London, and 75 ft. taller than the Statue of Liberty in New York Harbor.

We need trees because they take in carbon dioxide, which is present in our atmosphere naturally. But carbon dioxide is now at especially high levels because of burning fossil fuels, such as gas and coal. The high levels of carbon dioxide are warming the world and changing the climate. This is making ice melt and sea levels rise, and causing extreme weather. Trees are also home to birds and other wildlife, and over 80% of land animal species live in forests. So the more trees, the less carbon dioxide in our atmosphere and the more animals in the world.

SAVE the TREES

How many PLANET EARTHS FIT inside the SUN?

The Sun doesn't look all that big from here on Earth. But, as you've probably already figured out, that's because it's a really long way away. How much bigger is it than planet Earth, and just how far away is it?

I thought it would be BIGGER.

The volume of the Sun is about **338,000,000,000,000,000 cu. mi. (338 quadrillion cu. mi.).**

Earth's volume is about **260,000,000,000 cu. mi. (260 billion cu. mi.).**

About **1,300,000 EARTHS** would fit inside the Sun (you would have to reduce them to rubble and goo first, though).

TO WORK IT OUT

Divide 338,000,000,000,000,000 by **260,000,000,000** (there are too many zeros to fit on a calculator, so use the zero counting method on page 8.)

Our Sun is absolutely huge, but it's only medium-size as far as stars go—there are stars more than 100 times wider.

The smallest planet in our solar system is Mercury, which is about one-third the diameter of Earth.

SPACE TOURS

The Sun is our closest star. Earth and all the other planets in our solar system (eight altogether) are in orbit around it. In order from closest to the Sun, they are Mercury, Venus, Earth, Mars, Jupiter, Saturn, Uranus, and Neptune.

The Sun is about 93 million mi. away from Earth, which is known as an Astronomical Unit (AU). Sometimes scientists talk about very large distances in AUs.

The biggest planet is Jupiter, which is about 1,300 times bigger than Earth—in fact, all the other planets in the solar system could fit inside Jupiter. But you could still fit 1,000 Jupiters inside the Sun!

How Big is Earth?

Planet Earth is about 24,900 mi. measured all the way around the middle (its circumference). Traveling at 500 mph in a jet plane, it would take just under 50 hours to fly all the way around it.

The Sun's circumference measures about 2,700,000 mi. Traveling all the way around the Sun in a jet plane would take 225 days. If you lined up 109 planet Earths in a row, it would be equal to the diameter of the Sun.

How many SOCCER BALLS fill the World's BIGGEST STADIUM?

Have you ever wondered how many soccer balls would fill a stadium if you took out all the seats and locker rooms and things? Of course you have.

A soccer ball has a diameter of **8.65 in**. We're not going to squash the balls so there's no space between them, but if we just throw them in and allow them to nestle together, there will be about **101 soccer balls in 1 cubic yard (cu. yd.)**.

The biggest stadium in the world is Rungrado May Day Stadium in North Korea. Very roughly, its volume is **1,300,000 cu. yd. (1.3 million cu. yd.)**.

131,300,000 SOCCER BALLS would fill up the **WORLD'S BIGGEST STADIUM.**

TO WORK IT OUT

Multiply 1,300,000 by 101

Rungrado May Day Stadium in Pyongyang, North Korea, covers an area of 51 acres. Up to 114,000 people can fit into it to watch national celebrations and sporting events. The main field covers 242,200 sq. ft., and its scalloped roof (shaped to look like a magnolia flower) reaches almost 200 ft. high. No wonder it takes more than 130 million soccer balls to fill it.

Soccer is one of the most popular sports in the world. The soccer World Cup is probably the most watched sporting event—almost half of the entire population of the world watched at least some of the last one.

In Britain, women's soccer was banned from 1921 (when it was extremely popular) until 1971, because it wasn't seen as an appropriate sport for women! It's now enjoyed all over the world by millions of players and fans.

There are several stadiums in the world almost as big as the Rungrado May Day Stadium, all of them in the United States, and all of them used for football. The biggest is Michigan Stadium, with a crowd capacity of 111,000.

How many MICRORAPTORS make a TITANOSAUR?

Not all dinosaurs were huge lumbering monsters—these ancient beasts came in all sorts of shapes and sizes. How many of the smallest would weigh the same as the biggest?

Titanosaurs are the largest kind of dinosaur we know about. Ours weighed about **70 tons (or 140,000 lb.)**.

Microraptor, one of the smallest types of dinosaurs, weighed about **2 lb.**

70,000 MICRORAPTORS would weigh the same as ONE TITANOSAUR.

TO WORK IT OUT

Divide 140,000 by 2. This is an easy one!

There were different kinds of microraptors—little feathered dinosaurs about the size of crows that preyed on smaller animals. One of them, Microraptor gui, had feathers adapted for flight on all four of its limbs. It could probably fly, or at least glide.

Our big dinosaur is a titanosaur, a type of sauropod, which were huge planteaters. This titanosaur is a type called Argentinosaurus, which is thought to be not only the largest dinosaur, but the largest known land animal in the world ever. It measured 115 ft. from head to tail.

Elephants are the biggest land animals in the world today. Eleven of the very biggest African elephants would make one Argentinosaurus.

Compsognathus was one of the smallest nonflying dinosaurs—a little 25-in.-long meateater. It was about three times as heavy as a microraptor, so we'd need 23,300 or so of those to make one Argentinosaurus.

Microraptors and titanosaurs would never have met because they were separated by millions of years. Microraptors lived about 125 million years ago, while titanosaurs lived toward the end of the dinosaur age. Argentinosaurus lived around 90 million years ago.

The biggest meateating dinosaur fossil discovered so far is a Tyrannosaurus rex called Scotty, found in 2019. It measures 43 ft. long and would have weighed 19,400 lb. when it was alive—or 9,700 microraptors if you'd rather.

How many Central PARKS make the AMAZON RAIN FOREST?

The Amazon is the biggest tropical rain forest in the world, and it is very big indeed. Central Park in New York City is one of the most famous parks in the world. How many of one would fit inside the other?

Central Park is **1.3 sq. mi.**

The Amazon covers an area of about **2.1 million sq. mi.**

You could fit **1,615,384 AND A BIT CENTRAL PARKS INSIDE THE AMAZON RAIN FOREST.** Incidentally, the Amazon is roughly half the size of Europe.

TO WORK IT OUT
Divide 2,100,000 by 1.3

Most of the Amazon rain forest is in Brazil, but it covers parts of seven other countries in South America: Bolivia, Colombia, Ecuador, French Guiana, Guyana, Peru, and Suriname. Suriname is the smallest country in South America, at 63,250 sq. mi.—it could fit into the Amazon rain forest more than 30 times.

The Amazon is home to millions of different animals and plants. There are more than 2.5 million kinds of insects, more than 400 types of mammals, and thousands of types of fish and birds.

Tropical rain forests are hot and humid, with more than 6.5 ft. of rainfall per year and an average temperature higher than 82°F.

Among the extraordinary animals living in the Amazon are the world's biggest beetle, the titan beetle, and the world's smallest monkey, the pygmy marmoset.

Central Park includes a reservoir, a huge museum, a lake, various ponds and pools, a theater, a zoo, and even a castle. But obviously it's absolutely tiny compared to the world's biggest rain forest.

Rain forests are beautiful and also useful to the planet, because they absorb carbon dioxide and release oxygen, which helps stabilize the climate. Sadly, an area of the Amazon more than four and a half times the size of Suriname has been destroyed over the past 50 years, mostly to make way for grazing land for cattle.

How many ASTRONAUTS fit inside the INTERNATIONAL SPACE STATION?

The International Space Station (ISS) is in orbit about 250 mi. above Earth. How many astronauts are whizzing about up there with it, and how many more could fit inside?

The crew of the ISS is usually six astronauts. But what if we wanted to squash them in? We wouldn't really be that cruel, but just out of interest . . .

The ISS has a volume (where it's possible to live) of **13,696 cu. ft.**

An average astronaut takes up around **2.3 cu. ft.**

TO WORK IT OUT

Divide 13,696 by 2.3

5,954 ASTRONAUTS COULD FIT INSIDE THE INTERNATIONAL SPACE STATION. That's 5,948 more than the usual crew. Each bedroom would have to be shared by almost a thousand astronauts.

There have been astronauts living on the ISS since 2000. Peggy Whitson has spent the most time there —665 days.

The six astronauts on the ISS have a bedroom each. There are two bathrooms, a gym, and, of course, an absolutely amazing view, with a 360-degree bay window to see it from.

The ISS was set up in 1998 as a giant science lab in space. It measures about 358 ft. from end to end, travels at 5 mi. per second, and orbits Earth 16 times every 24 hours.

Altogether, more than 230 astronauts from 18 different countries have visited the International Space Station. Not all at once, though!

There's hardly any gravity, so the astronauts float everywhere and have to work out in the gym for two hours a day to make up for it. They sleep strapped into sleeping bags on the walls, and when they go to the bathroom they strap themselves in to make sure there's no chance of anything escaping. The waste is sucked away.

HOW Many goldfish make a BLUE WHALE?

Blue whales are the biggest animals that have ever existed on Earth. Obviously, goldfish are teeny tiny by comparison. But how many of these little guys would weigh the same as a whopping great blue whale?

A blue whale can weigh up to **200 tons**, or 6,400,000 (6.4 million) ounces.

Goldfish vary in size, but ours, named Graham, weighs **16 ounces**.

400,000 GOLDFISH like Graham would weigh the same as one blue whale!

🧮 TO WORK IT OUT

Divide 6,400,000 by 16

Often goldfish are kept in small tanks, but if they're given a nice big tank to swim around in, they'll grow bigger and be happier.

You can tell a blue whale's age from its earwax. Around every six months, a new layer of earwax forms. These earplugs tell scientists that blue whales usually live between 80 to 90 years. The oldest on record lived about 110 years.

Blue whales eat tiny creatures called krill—up to four tons of them a day. Goldfish will eat almost anything, including their own poop. They will keep eating and eating, because they don't have a stomach and can't tell when they're full.

ALL YOU CAN EAT!

When a blue whale is born, it already weighs almost 2 tons, or 4,000 goldfish. When it's fully grown, it measures up to 100 ft. long—200 Graham-sized goldfish could line up along it.

A blue whale's tongue weighs as much as a rhinoceros, and its heart is the size of a car.

Goldfish are freshwater fish, so they woudn't meet a blue whale in real life. They're a type of carp, originally from east Asia.

Goldfish are famous for only being able to remember things for a few seconds, but that's not true. They can identify shapes, colors, and sounds, and they can be taught to do tricks like pushing balls through hoops.

The world's biggest known goldfish weighed 2 lb. and measured 12.5 in., but most don't reach anywhere near that size.

HOW MANY SOCCER FIELDS to cover PLANET EARTH?

The last time you watched an especially exciting World Cup match, you were probably wondering just how many of those fields it would take to cover the entire planet. In between goals, obviously.

The surface area of Earth is about **197,000,000 (197 million) sq. mi.** A lot of that is under the sea, so if we're talking about dry land, the area is about **57 million sq. mi.**

Soccer fields can be different sizes, but ours measures 130 yd. long by 75 yd. wide, which is an area of **9,750 sq. yd.**, or **0.0031 sq. mi.**

We'd need almost **63,548,387,097** of our **SOCCER FIELDS TO COVER ALL OF PLANET EARTH.**

TO COVER THE WORLD'S DRY LAND, we would need **18,387,096,774** (and a bit) of our soccer fields.

🖩 TO WORK IT OUT

Divide 197,000,000 by 0.0031
To work it out for just the land area **divide 57,000,000 by 0.0031**

Earth's crust is made up of great big chunks called tectonic plates. Millions of years ago, the plates were all joined together in one huge supercontinent. Then they drifted apart, and made mountains as they crashed together again.

How Many Soccer Fields Would Cover . . .

THE ENTIRE OCEAN: 45,161,290,323

THE WORLD'S LARGEST LAKE: (Caspian Sea) 46,207,710

THE WORLD'S BIGGEST COUNTRY: (Russia) 2,129,570,369

THE WORLD'S SMALLEST COUNTRY: (the Vatican) You'd need just 54.8 soccer fields, because the Vatican is really very small indeed.

Some Soccer Numbers . . .

There are more countries with soccer teams than any other sport—there are 211 national men's teams, and 176 national women's teams. Soccer is the most popular team sport played by women.

Jetpack JOURNEYS

By this stage in the book, you are probably wondering what on earth has happened to the jetpack you were promised. At last, here it is! Put it on and get ready to fly to destinations around the world—and beyond—at 500 mph.

You might have already flown at 500 mph—passenger planes often reach that speed.

Cross-country Journeys:

ACROSS CANADA FROM EAST TO WEST (widest point): 11.75 hours

ACROSS CHINA FROM EAST TO WEST (widest point): 6.5 hours

ACROSS THE UNITED STATES FROM EAST TO WEST (widest point): 5.5 hours

ACROSS BRAZIL FROM EAST TO WEST (widest point): 5.25 hours

ACROSS MAINLAND ITALY FROM NORTH TO SOUTH (widest point): 1.5 hours

City to City Journeys:

NEW YORK, NY, TO LONDON, UK: 6.75 hours

DELHI, INDIA, TO SYDNEY, AUSTRALIA: 13 hours

BEIJING, CHINA, TO PARIS, FRANCE: 10.25 hours

LAGOS, NIGERIA, TO PRETORIA, SOUTH AFRICA: 5.5 hours

BERLIN, GERMANY, TO LOS ANGELES, CA: 11.5 hours

Journeys around the World:

WORLD'S LONGEST RAILROAD (THE TRANS-SIBERIAN RAILROAD): 11.5 hours

THE GREAT WALL OF CHINA: 26.5 hours

THE RIVER NILE: 8.5 hours

THE PACIFIC OCEAN (FROM EAST TO WEST AT WIDEST POINT): 24.5 hours

THE ATLANTIC OCEAN: 8 hours

Space Journeys from Earth to:

THE MOON: 18 days and 6 hours

MARS (AT CLOSEST POINT): 7 years and 264 days

THE SUN: 21 years and 77 days

JUPITER (AT CLOSEST POINT): 89 years and 30 days

NEPTUNE (AT CLOSEST POINT): 609 years and 83 days

Measuring in Metric

By Kjartan Poskitt

Metric measurements are often used in science and math, because they are based on multiples of 10, which makes calculations and comparisons simpler.

In the metric system, the base unit is 1 meter (which you can write as 1 m). We use meters for measuring lines or distances. 1 m is about as long as a belt or the height of a table top.

There are 100 centimeters (100 cm) in 1 meter.
1 cm is about the width of a pea.

There are 1,000 millimeters (1,000 mm) in 1 meter. 1 mm is about the thickness of ten pieces of paper.

1,000 meters = 1 kilometer (or 1 km). That's about as far as you can walk in 10 minutes.

If we need to measure the size of areas such as a carpet or the surface of Earth, we can use square meters (m²) or square kilometers (km²) for big areas.

1 meter

1 meter | 1 meter

A square with sides a meter long is 1 square meter (1 m²).

1 meter

One square meter (1 m²) is about half the size of a door in an ordinary house.

One square centimeter (1 cm²) is about the size of your little fingernail.

1 meter

One square millimeter (1 mm²) is about the size of a big period.

1 meter — **1 meter**

1 meter

A cube with sides a meter long is 1 cubic meter (1 m³).

If we need to know the size of chunky things such as soccer balls or elephants, we can measure their volume in cubic meters (m³). One cubic meter is about the size of a big washing machine.

One cubic millimeter (1 mm³) is the size of a grain of sugar.

One cubic centimeter (1 cm³) is the size of a small die.

Index

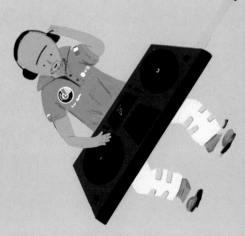

Answers to page 9:
One year = about 31.5 million seconds

1,000,000 ants = 6,560 ft., 100 giraffes = 1,640 ft.

Eiffel Tower = 11,000 tons, pool water = 2,755 tons